C000140457

Old Dog's
Guide for Pups

Old Dog's Guide for Pups

*Advice and Rules for
Human Training*

Allen Appel
and
Mike Rothmiller

ST. MARTIN'S PRESS ※ NEW YORK

www.stmartins.com

Design by Nancy Resnick

Library of Congress Cataloging-in-Publication Data

Appel, Allen.
    Old dog's guide for pups : advice and rules for human
training / Allen Appel and Mike Rothmiller.--1st ed.
        p. cm.
    ISBN 0-312-26212-4
    1. Dogs—Humor. I. Rothmiller, Mike. II. Title.

PN6231.D68 A66 2000
818'.5402--dc21   00-035252

First Edition: October 2000

10 9 8 7 6 5 4 3 2 1

This book is dedicated to a great human, Konrad Lorenz. This is what he had to say about dogs:

"The fidelity of a dog is a precious gift demanding no less binding moral responsibilities than the friendship of a human being. A bond with a true dog is as lasting as the ties of this earth can ever be."

Old Dog's
Guide for Pups

Introduction

Old Dog

Okay, you pups out there, listen up. Old Dog is about to Explain It All. Everything. The Whole Bone.

Commonsense Human Training is as simple as one, two, three. Once you grasp our Three Basic Principles, you're on your way to a Dog's

Life. Train your human to supply the Three Great Needs and you'll breeze through from pup to Old Dog with barely a NoNoNo along the way. Then at the end of a long day you can lie down, give a contented sigh, and go to sleep, a Happy Dog.

Actually, there's a fourth Need, a great overarching principle, but we'll get to that at the end. That's where it will make the most sense. Right now let's apply the lessons learned from fifty thousand years of human domestication. We've taken them from caves to condos, from dinosaurs to dog doors, and if you apply this accumulation of Canine Wisdom you too can own, train, and enjoy the Perfect Human.

Chapter 1

The Three Great Needs

Here it is, pups, the great Triumvirate of a dog's life, the Basic Pleasures, the Golden Three:

> Playing
> Eating
> Sleeping

The only thing that changes as you grow is the order of events. Right now play is first; when you hit your teens and adult years, food takes top position; when you achieve Old Dog status, sleeping in all its glorious forms becomes your main concern. But whatever order you're interested in, the purpose of Human Training is to satisfy these all-important needs.

There will be times when you will think that you're never going to get your human trained. You'll think of him or her as little more than a former tree ape who has, through sheer dumb luck, access to can openers, cars, and cable TV. A species that has had the great good fortune to develop opposable thumbs and the ability to walk upright. But don't be discouraged. Sure, we can't drive, but what's so bad about having a human to do all the work while you hang your head out the window and feel the wind in your ears?

Remember: You Are Not Alone. Old Dog Is Here.

Chapter 2

Playing

Sometimes it's hard for a young pup to remember what belongs to you, and what belongs to the human. Commit the following Ten Commandments of Toys to memory. Repeat them over and over until they are part of your very soul:

1. Everything is a toy.
2. If it's on the floor, it's a toy.

3. If it's on the floor, it's mine.
4. If it's in my mouth, it's mine. And you can't have it back.
5. If I can get it away from you, it's mine.
6. If I've got it chewed up, all the pieces are mine.
7. If it's under the bed, it's mine.
8. If it's a ball, it's mine. All of them. You can throw it and I'll chase it, but you can't have it back unless I want you to throw it again. The same applies to the flat flying thing.
9. If I can carry it, tug on it, chew it, or bury it, it's a toy. And it's mine.
10. If it's a sock, it's mine. But you can wear it first for a while.

The trick is to remember that what the human sees as "Training the Dog" is really play.

Basic Rule: Everything is a game.

Eleven Amusing Responses to Training Commands:

1. Sit (unless commanded to sit)
2. Stare
3. Cock head slightly while staring, as if agreeable but puzzled
4. Yawn
5. Walk away
6. Lick privates
7. Bark
8. Scratch head with rear leg
9. Lie down and go to sleep
10. Pee on nearby object
11. Run and find your ball or Frisbee, place it at your human's feet, and bark

Basic Rule: Remember, staring is one of the strongest weapons in a dog's arsenal. If simple staring doesn't get that desired toy or piece of food, move closer. Keep moving closer until you get what you want. Never give up. When you're as close as you can get, breathe with your mouth open on your human's face. Finally, they will understand and give you the attention you deserve.

Three Classic Games:

1. Chase the human and jump up on them. (Muddy paws are a nice plus here.)
2. Human chases the dog around the neighborhood. (If you've escaped from the house or yard, so much the better.)
3. Chase the human on the bicycle. Barking makes them go even faster.

Nine Great Things to Chase, besides Humans:

1. Cats. Always cats.

2. Birds
3. Balls (though only if someone has thrown them)
4. Squirrels
5. Otherdogs
6. Your tail
7. Blowing leaves
8. Your shadow
9. The wind

Two Things That Are Fun to Chase but Not
Fun to Catch:

1. Skunks

2. Porcupines

If you find something that was once alive but is now dead, especially if has been dead for a long time, roll in it. The fun in this will become quickly apparent when you walk into the house and greet your human.

Squeaky toys are fun to chew on. Make sure you sit near your human and make the squeaky sound over and over. And over. (For advice on how to eat these toys, see the chapter on eating.)

Eight Things That Must Always Be Barked At:

1. The mailman
2. Anyone in any sort of uniform
3. Otherdogs
4. Humans in funny hats
5. The vacuum cleaner
6. Animals on television

7. The pizza guy
8. Mirrors

Howling at sirens is always fulfilling.

❧

Howling along with your human is fun and makes them happy.

Flowers are always good to dig up and chew. When you're a pup you can usually get away with this.

When you're a puppy, a shoe is the best toy. When you're a little older you'll appreciate a broader assortment. (See Toy Commandments pp. 7–8.)

When given a new toy, make it your favorite for a few days. Then ignore it. A new toy will soon appear.

❧

Toilet paper is fun to unroll, and good to eat.

❧

The Number One Most Fun Thing of All Time:

Put your nose in their crotch. This is especially amusing if the human is female.

To him you're fetching the newspaper. To you it's a game of tug of war.

Three Extremely Fun but Very Dangerous
Things to Do:

1. Chase cars.

2. Pretend that you are trying to cross a busy
   highway. Start, stop, then go back. Do this
   over and over.
3. Run away from home.

Basic Rule: When a human attempts to call your attention to something by pointing at it, always stare at the finger rather than the thing being pointed at.

If you wag your tail hard enough, they'll play with you.

Basic Rule: After a bath, run around and act crazy. If you're in the house, roll all over the rugs. If you're outside, roll in the grass or in the dirt. This is one of the cardinal rules of being a dog.

Don't let one of the little humans give you a haircut. This is not fun.

Six Things to Do When Riding in the Car:

1. If the window is closed, press your nose against the glass and breathe deeply until the glass is all wet and smeary.
2. If the window is open, stick your head out as far as it will go.
3. Bark at all other cars, trucks, dogs, people, or anything else that goes by outside.
4. Shed all over the seat covers.
5. Lick the driver's ear unexpectedly while the car is in motion.
6. Vomit in the backseat.

Play fetch with the ball until your human is exhausted. Never give up first.

Occasionally bark insanely at the window even though there is nothing really there.

Learn a good growl, for when things get too rough when you are playing. A good growl means, "Whatever You Are Doing Right Now, Stop It!"

A dog is always ready to play.

Always greet guests by leaping on them. The only reason they have come to visit is to see you.

Make sure you ready tennis balls for play by chewing on them until they are slick with spit.

Push open the door and stare at humans while they are "doing their business."

Going on a trip is always more fun than staying home.

Stand quietly and stare at humans while they are mating. Eventually they will notice you.

Always bring dead animals in from outside and leave them on the good rug. Chew them a little first.

The more kids you can find to play with, the better.

It's hard to believe, but not everyone wants to play.

Ten Things They Want You to Wear That Are
Not Fun:

1. Dog sweaters or coats
2. T-shirts
3. Bandanas
4. Stupid-looking antlers at Christmas
5. Doggie slippers and shoes
6. Doggie diapers
7. Christmas bells
8. Anything at Halloween
9. Ribbons around your neck or head
10. Sunglasses

Some tricks are just not worth doing.

You know you're capable of much more than they think you are, but it's not necessarily a good idea to let them know just how much you could do if you really wanted to.

Twelve Words That Always Mean Fun:

1. Treat
2. Goforaride
3. Goforawalk
4. Gooddog!
5. Dinner
6. Ball
7. Catch
8. Frisbee
9. We're home
10. Gotothepark
11. Goforarun
12. Get the kitty

It may not be a car, but it's still fun.

Run! The faster, the better.

Fifteen Words That *Never* Mean Fun:

1. Vet
2. Bad Dog
3. Neutering
4. Fixed
5. Shots
6. Drop it!
7. Out!
8. No!
9. Stop that whining
10. Cut it out
11. I mean it
12. Dog pound
13. Bath
14. Medicine
15. %##!&&*###!!!

For all you males out there, leg humping is lots of fun, but if you act like you care for it too much your human might take you to the vet (I can hardly say these words) and have you "fixed." Oh, God, what do they think needs fixing!

Eight Things to Do on a Rainy Day:

1. Chew up the TV remote
2. Root through the laundry
3. Turn over food bowl
4. Eat tissues
5. Eat the mail
6. Tear up the carpet
7. Chew up soft drink cans and leave the pieces all over the place
8. Nap, eat, nap, eat, whine to go outside, nap, eat; continue until rain is over

Old dogs *can* learn new tricks, they just don't see any point to it.

The more dogs you can get barking at the same time, the more fun it is.

Sixty percent of all humans are overweight. It's in their best interest to get out in the backyard and play hard.

It's all in the attitude. If you're going to get your human to play, you've got to look like you're ready to play.

Getting wet. Never go out in the rain if they want you to, but always go out in the rain if they don't want you to. And playing with the hose is always fun, unless it involves getting a bath.

Whenever your human stands up, it means they're going to take you out and play with you. Act accordingly.

When playing, no doesn't really mean *No!* unless it's said three times, and even then it might mean yes if you're persistent.

Size doesn't matter. Little guys have just as much fun as big guys.

If you're bored, push your ball somewhere you can't get at it, then bark like crazy until someone comes to help.

Sneezing in your human's face is fun. Watch them jump!

Three fun places to get stuck:

1. Under the bed
2. Under the porch
3. Under the car

An enterprising pup can find at least a bit of fun in almost any situation except those involving veterinarians.

There is no right or wrong when playing.

Two fun gifts to give to your human:

1. Dead animals
2. Dirty underwear you get out of the
   hamper

It is possible to play with some cats, but who would want to?

Jumping into the pool is fun. Falling into the pool is not fun.

Anything with wheels should be chased.

Ⓐ

If you only had access to their equipment, think how much fun you could have!

Some dogs think watching television is fun, some don't. There's no accounting for taste.

Two things that are not fun:

1. Earthquakes
2. Fireworks

Stuffed toy dogs are fun. Tear them apart and scatter the pieces all over the house.

You'll find plenty of humans to play with at a school. But mind your manners.

Can't get your human to play? Get your tennis ball good and wet with spit. Press it against your human's bare leg. Watch them jump. (This doesn't work if they're wearing long pants.)

✦

A fence is the enemy of fun.

No toys to play with? The stick is a classic: easy to play with, always fun, always available.

If it feels good, do it.

Chapter 3

Eating

Dog food is anything a dog decides to eat.

Always gulp your food.

Seven Commandments of Food:

1. Any food on the floor belongs to the dog.
2. Begging is not demeaning if it gets results.
3. The worst of their food is better than the best of our food.
4. Sit near the young ones, they drop the most food.
5. Pretty much anything is good to eat, especially if it was once alive.
6. Pretty much anything is good to eat if it can be broken into swallowable pieces.
7. If it tastes good, eat it. You can always throw it up later.

Basic Rule: Any water found other than in the dog's water bowl will be better water than that found in the dog's water bowl.

Best not to share your food with any of the locals. Some guys will always take advantage of your generosity.

Squeaky toys and rubber toys in general are good to eat but, as noted in the preceding Commandments, must be chewed first into small pieces. Swallowing the squeaker thing is up to the individual dog.

Stealing large food items off the table will get you into serious trouble, but it is probably worth it.

Some food jokes are not funny.

Show your appreciation when you get special treats.

Somebody, somewhere, started the rumor that real bones were bad for dogs. That person should be killed.

❧

Turtles would be good to eat if you could just chew through the shell.

The Seven Greatest Things to Eat:

1. Real bones
2. Meat
3. Ice cream
4. All fast food
5. Anything fried
6. Ice cubes
7. Small live animals

Seven Great Places to Get a Drink:

1. Toilet
2. Hose
3. Swimming pools
4. Puddle
5. Otherdogs' water bowl
6. The gutter
7. A little human's cup

Grass is always fun to eat. Everyone gets excited when you do.

Old lady humans don't run and play much, but their chow is usually excellent and they share freely.

Be patient. Bide your time. Humans always drop or spill something.

Eight More Great Things to Eat:

1. Candy wrappers
2. Candy in general (go easy on the choco-late)
3. Things run over in the road
4. Unidentifiable junk found while on a walk
5. Your own vomit
6. Toilet paper
7. Used tissues
8. Anything that smells good

That thing humans do where they balance your treat on your nose before allowing you to eat it is not funny, even if they think it is. If you "accidentally on purpose" give their fingers a little nip when they attempt it they will soon stop.

Basic Rule: All dog biscuits are good, but they'll never equal a dried pig's ear.

The container called "the garbage" is where they keep lots of great food. Garbage cans are meant to be opened and emptied.

For a different taste treat, try the neighbor's garbage. They put this out for you one or two times a week in white or green plastic bags. Rip 'em open and chow down!

Doing tricks for treats is not demeaning if the treats are good enough.

If you keep after the fussy-eater thing with enough persistence eventually you'll be eating their food. They'll never let you starve, no matter what they say.

Stand near them when they cook. They always drop good food on the floor.

Five Things You Should Never Eat:

1. Slugs
2. Wires
3. Mothballs (moths are fine)
4. Razors
5. Cigarette butts

Your human thinks that since you have your own food, you shouldn't want their food. This is crazy. Have they ever actually *tasted* your food?

Snow is good to eat, but you can eat a ton of it and all it does is make you pee.

Resist *all* food changes, unless moving up to a better class of food.

Always expect a treat for doing a trick. Teach your human that there are no free rides.

Dirt soup is not good to eat, even if it sounds like it might be.

Bars of soap taste pretty good and are interesting to eat.

They always drop at least one kernel of popcorn. Usually more.

Never lick a frog. They taste terrible.

Another good source of water is the aquarium. That's the water bowl with the little swimming things in it.

If they're eating, you should be eating.

Sometimes the really little humans will drink from your water bowl. That's okay, you won't catch anything.

Ice cubes are good to eat, good to chase around the floor, and good to have in your water bowl on a hot day. But don't bother burying them for later.

In fact, burying anything is probably a lost cause. Most dogs can't remember where bones are buried, but it's fun to dig the hole and cover them up.

🐾

Almost everything even vaguely shaped like a bone is okay to chew.

Holidays mean an abundance of special treats:

HALLOWEEN: candy; candy wrappers
CHRISTMAS: tinsel; pine needles; package wrappings

EASTER: plastic grass; unfound Easter eggs; live pet bunnies!
THANKSGIVING: the whole turkey—if you've got the guts to get up on the table and get it

Little humans drop the most food.

There's always a lot of good leftovers for you to lick off the faces of the *really* little ones.

The Lord helps them who help themselves.

Two Great Things about Cat Food:

1. It tastes perfectly good.
2. Cats usually leave some behind in their bowl for later.

More Stuff That Is *Not* Good to Eat:

    Cat litter
    The TV remote (though this makes an
       excellent chew toy)
    Pens or markers (they mess up your face)
    Drywall
    Most construction materials
    Hot peppers

More Stuff That Is *Good* to Eat:

> Most houseplants
> Charcoal
> Garbage juice
> Crickets
> Dead mice
> Live mice

It's worth it to learn at least a few words of their language.

FEEDING TIME!

Be Alert for the Following Sounds, They Often Mean Possible Food:

> Refrigerator door opening
> Kitchen cabinet door being opened
> Can opener
> Trash can being opened
> Cellophane being crinkled

Lick everything. You can never tell when food might be involved.

Coffee. Sneak it when you can. It's black, bitter, and good. But drink too much and it makes you feel weird.

Never drink antifreeze, even though it tastes good. Trust me.

All dog treats are good, regardless of size, color, or brand. Some are better than others, but all are good.

Good dogs deserve good bones.

Books, newspapers, and magazines can be eaten, but they don't taste very good. The fun is in the chewing.

Eating a long piece of string can be interesting when it comes out your butt. Your human will then chase you around the yard for hours trying to retrieve the string. No one knows why they do this.

•

While your human is explaining to you why you shouldn't be eating something, try to look as if you care. It makes them feel better.

Chew bones, don't swallow them.

Peanut butter stuffed in a bone tastes great, but it will drive you crazy trying to get at it.

Sometimes they try to hide a pill in a spoonful of peanut butter. Carefully lick up the peanut butter and leave the pill behind.

A small amount of alcoholic leftover drinks is okay, but don't make a habit of it.

—————————— 🐾 ——————————

Empty pizza boxes are quite tasty.

🐾

If it fits in your mouth, it is food. Or at least it has food potential.

Chapter 4

Sleeping

Ten Great Places to Sleep, in Order of Preference:

1. Her bed
2. His bed
3. Their bed
4. The kid's bed
5. On cool tile (in the summer)

6. In front of the heating grate (in the winter)
7. Anywhere you're in the way
8. On the couch or chair (if forbidden)
9. Snuggled up on or against a human
10. In the dog bed

When sleeping try to twitch your feet every once in a while and make small whiny noises. For some reason this amuses humans and they will often give you a treat for it.

Basic Rule: Any place they get to sleep is better than any place you're supposed to sleep.

Your job is to get into their bed. Your best tool is to Look Sad. This is accomplished by holding the head slightly downward and looking up with the eyes.

Head cocked to the side is optional.

Once you're on the bed or chair, use your Sad Look to stay there.

If you can't get into their bed or their chair while they're in it, wait until they leave. If they're not there, they can't keep you off.

If you look cute enough, you can sleep anywhere you want.

When sleeping on the human's bed, always get onto their spot when they get up. It will be nice and warm.

When sleeping against a human, pretend to be asleep when they attempt to push you away. Soon they will tire of this and stop bothering you.

Pups need twenty hours of sleep a day. Sleep anywhere,

and often.

Old Dogs are allowed to sleep anywhere, and as often as they like. They've earned it.

Sleeping together is even nicer than sleeping alone.

The trick to sleeping on their furniture is persistence. If you get up on a chair or couch every time possible, and do this over and over, they will eventually designate this piece of furniture as "the dog's chair." As soon as this happens, start getting up on another piece of furniture. Someday the whole house will be yours.

If your human is sleeping and you're bored, stand by the bed and whine softly. Soon they will arise and take you outside, even if it's the middle of the night.

Six Great Things to Sleep On:

1. Their clothing
2. Blankets; drag them off the bed
3. Anything they leave on the floor
4. Your human's feet
5. A lap
6. Clean clothes in the laundry basket

The Greatest Sleeping Spot in All the World:

In front of the fireplace. (As long as there's a fire.)

After a few years, if you are sleeping when the human arrives home it is not necessary to leap up to greet them.

Farting while sleeping is not your fault. In fact farting in general is never your fault.

Always circle in place three times before settling down to sleep. No dog knows why we do this, but it's tradition, so keep it up. The Old Ways are important.

If possible, always sleep in the sun.

Your human will feel guilty when you lie around and sleep all day. This is good as they will then play with you. Don't ever let them find out that we enjoy sleeping all day.

When Old Dog is sleeping, do not bother him.

Sleeping fills the time nicely between playing and eating.

When they leave you alone, just go to sleep. They'll come back, they always do.

Sometimes your human will twitch and moan while they are sleeping. They are dreaming about chasing cats.

Sometimes both your humans will put you in the hall, close the bedroom door, and twitch and moan while they are sleeping. They are both dreaming about chasing cats.

Try not to bother your human at night when they are sleeping unless it's really important or you notice something that should be brought to their attention or you're bored.

❧

It is fine to wake your human if it is daytime. Daytime technically begins when the first photon of light creeps in around the window shade.

Chapter 5

Putting It All Together; the Fourth Need

Love thy human.

It doesn't get much simpler than this. Dog and man have been bound together for thousands of years by the twin bonds of love and respect. The pact has been elemental, and indestructible: the humans fulfill our needs, in return we give them absolute loyalty and unconditional love. And if any man lifts a hand to any dog, or any dog bares a tooth to any human, the fabric of trust weakens and both species are the less for it.

Dogs have a responsibility as well as humans, because in the end, both are equal. To those who have entered into the bond, there is no difference: the passing of a beloved human is no more, nor less, than the passing of a beloved dog. In life, and death, they are friends, comrades, and equals.